WHOLE WIDE WORLD
PYRAMIDS OF GIZA

by Kristine Spanier, MLIS

Ideas for Parents and Teachers

Pogo Books let children practice reading informational text while introducing them to nonfiction features such as headings, labels, sidebars, maps, and diagrams, as well as a table of contents, glossary, and index.

Carefully leveled text with a strong photo match offers early fluent readers the support they need to succeed.

Before Reading

- "Walk" through the book and point out the various nonfiction features. Ask the student what purpose each feature serves.
- Look at the glossary together. Read and discuss the words.

Read the Book

- Have the child read the book independently.
- Invite him or her to list questions that arise from reading.

After Reading

- Discuss the child's questions. Talk about how he or she might find answers to those questions.
- Prompt the child to think more. Ask: Pyramids were built as tombs to honor Egyptian pharaohs. What other structures do you know of that honor leaders?

Pogo Books are published by Jump!
5357 Penn Avenue South
Minneapolis, MN 55419
www.jumplibrary.com

Library of Congress Cataloging-in-Publication Data

Names: Spanier, Kristine, author. | Spanier, Kristine. Whole wide world.
Title: Pyramids of Giza / by Kristine Spanier, MLIS.
Description: Minneapolis: Jump!, Inc. [2022]
Series: Whole wide world
Includes index. | Audience: Ages 7-10
Identifiers: LCCN 2021031456 (print)
LCCN 2021031457 (ebook)
ISBN 9781636903163 (hardcover)
ISBN 9781636903170 (paperback)
ISBN 9781636903187 (ebook)
Subjects: LCSH: Pyramids—Egypt—Jīzah—Juvenile literature. Great Pyramid (Egypt)—Juvenile literature.
Classification: LCC DT63 .S63 2022 (print)
LCC DT63 (ebook) | DDC 932/.012—dc23
LC record available at https://lccn.loc.gov/2021031456
LC ebook record available at https://lccn.loc.gov/2021031457

Editor: Jenna Gleisner
Designer: Molly Ballanger

Photo Credits: Dan Breckwoldt/Shutterstock, cover; Eric Valenne geostory/Shutterstock, 1; Marti Bug Catcher/Shutterstock, 3; Whatafoto/Shutterstock, 4; ImAAm/Shutterstock, 5, 6-7; Daniel Samray/Shutterstock, 8-9; nodostudio/iStock, 10; Peacefoo/iStock, 11; Dorling Kindersley/Getty, 12-13t; LexyLovesArt/iStock, 12-13b; robertharding/Alamy, 14-15; Graham Prentice/Alamy, 16-17; Tips Images/SuperStock, 18; Diego Fiore/iStock, 19; Kateryna Kolesnyk/Getty, 20-21; TanaCh/Shutterstock, 23.

Printed in the United States of America at Corporate Graphics in North Mankato, Minnesota.

TABLE OF CONTENTS

CHAPTER 1

SIX PYRAMIDS

Egypt has more than 100 **ancient** pyramids. Near the city of Giza, six of them are grouped together. These are the Pyramids of Giza.

Great
Pyramid

Pharaohs once ruled Egypt. Khufu was the ruler more than 4,500 years ago. He ordered a large pyramid to be built. It would be his **tomb**. It is one of the six Pyramids of Giza. It is called the Great Pyramid. It is the largest in Egypt.

A smaller pyramid was built next to it. It was for Khufu's son Khafre. Another was built for his grandson Menkaure. Three smaller pyramids sit in front. These were for Khufu's wives.

Pyramid of Khafre

Pyramid of Menkaure

TAKE A LOOK!

How big are the three main Pyramids of Giza? Take a look!

449 feet (137 meters) — HEIGHT

GREAT PYRAMID

WIDTH — **755 feet (230 meters)**

449 feet (137 meters) — HEIGHT

PYRAMID OF KHAFRE

WIDTH — **707 feet (215 meters)**

213 feet (65 meters) — HEIGHT

PYRAMID OF MENKAURE

WIDTH — **358 feet (109 meters)**

The Great Sphinx is here, too.
It is 66 feet (20 m) tall. It is
240 feet (73 m) long.

Its face looks like Khafre.
But it has the body of a lion.
Why? Lions were **symbols**
of **royalty**.

CHAPTER 2

THE GREAT PYRAMID

It took more than 20 years to build the Great Pyramid. More than 20,000 people worked on it. It is made of granite. This stone came from **quarries**. Boats carried it down the Nile River.

Nile River

More than 2 million granite blocks make up the Great Pyramid. Each one weighs as much as two elephants! Workers probably used ropes to pull the blocks up ramps to stack them.

Great Pyramid
then

capstone

Great Pyramid
now

The Great Pyramid looked much different when it was first built. Limestone covered the outside. This stone would have looked bright in the sunshine. **Earthquakes** shook the limestone loose long ago. Some of the granite has worn away.

A capstone formed the point. It was shaped like a triangle. People believe it was made of gold.

DID YOU KNOW?

The Great Pyramid's capstone is missing. What happened to it? No one knows!

Three main rooms are inside. The Grand **Gallery** is first. It leads to the other two rooms. The Queen's **Chamber** probably stored treasures.

Khufu's **sarcophagus** is in the King's Chamber. Today it is empty. No one knows what happened to his **mummy**.

WHAT DO YOU THINK?

Pyramids were not built for people to go inside. They are tight. There is not much fresh air. Would you like to go inside one? Why or why not?

Grand Gallery

Pharaohs believed they would be gods after death. They were buried with things they wanted to take with them.

Pieces of a boat were found in the King's Chamber. Khufu may have believed he could use the boat in the **afterlife**. It has been rebuilt for people to see.

WHAT DO YOU THINK?

Pharaohs were buried with many treasures. Khufu's were stolen long ago. What else do you think may have been in his tomb?

CHAPTER 3

THE PYRAMIDS TODAY

Today, we can visit and go inside the pyramids. People from around the world come to see them.

The entrance to the Great Pyramid is very small. It wasn't always there. Robbers made the hole more than 1,200 years ago! They used it to sneak inside.

entrance • • • • ▶

The Pyramids of Giza are a treasure. They have stood for thousands of years. Would you like to visit?

QUICK FACTS & TOOLS

AT A GLANCE

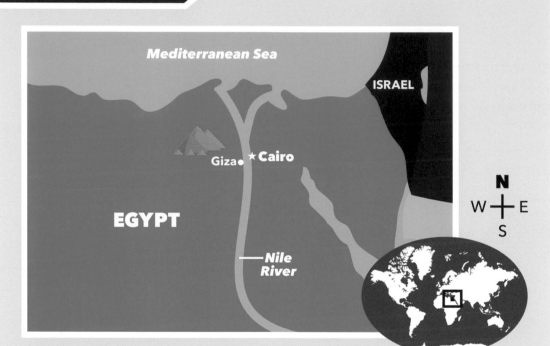

Mediterranean Sea

ISRAEL

Giza● ★Cairo

EGYPT

—Nile River

N
W ┼ E
S

PYRAMIDS OF GIZA

Location: Giza, Egypt

Years Built: 2550 to 2490 BCE

Past Use: tombs of pharaohs and other royalty

Current Use: cultural site and visitor attraction

Number of Visitors Each Year: up to 15 million

afterlife: An existence after death.

ancient: Belonging to a period long ago.

chamber: An enclosed space or room.

earthquakes: Sudden, violent shakings of Earth that may damage buildings and cause injuries.

gallery: A long and narrow passage.

mummy: A dead body that has been preserved with special chemicals and wrapped in cloth.

pharaohs: Kings of ancient Egypt.

quarries: Places where stone, slate, or sand is taken from Earth.

royalty: A king or queen or members of his or her family.

sarcophagus: A stone coffin from ancient times.

symbols: Objects that stand for, suggest, or represent something else.

tomb: A grave, room, or building for holding a dead body.

TO LEARN MORE

Finding more information is as easy as 1, 2, 3.

1 Go to www.factsurfer.com

2 Enter "PyramidsofGiza" into the search box.

3 Choose your book to see a list of websites.

FACT SURFER